THE PORTAGE POETRY SERIES

SERIES TITLES

Users with Access: New and Selected Poems
Brandon Krieg

Flu Season
Katie Kalisz

No Trouble Staying Awake
Teresa Scollon

Another Native Tongue
Susan Riley Clarke

Catch & Release
Lauren Crawford

Steelhead
Lauren K. Carlson

The Coronation of the Ghost
Benjamin Gantcher

The Stone Tries to Understand the Hands
Susannah Sheffer

Red Camaro
Dwaine Rieves

Where Babies Come From
Ori Fienberg

Cuttings
Hannah Dow

Forgive the Animal
Sarah Pape

Love as Invasive Species
Ellen Kombiyil

They Were Horrible Cooks
Allison Whittenberg

The New Life
Wendy Wisner

Restoring Prairie
Margaret Rozga

Table with Burning Candle
Julia Paul

A Bright Wound
Sarah A. Etlinger

The Velvet Book
Rae Gouirand

Listening to Mars
Sally Ashton

Glitter City
Bonnie Jill Emanuel

Bone Country
Linda Nemec Foster

Not Just the Fire
R.B. Simon

Monarch
Heather Bourbeau

The Walk to Cefalù
Lynne Viti

The Found Object Imagines a Life: New and Selected Poems
Mary Catherine Harper

Naming the Ghost
Emily Hockaday

Mourning
Dokubo Melford Goodhead

Messengers of the Gods: New and Selected Poems
Kathryn Gahl

After the 8-Ball
Colleen Alles

Careful Cartography
Devon Bohm

Broken On the Wheel
Barbara Costas-Biggs

Sparks and Disperses
Cathleen Cohen

Holding My Selves Together: New and Selected Poems
Margaret Rozga

Lost and Found Departments
Heather Dubrow

Marginal Notes
Alfonso Brezmes

The Almost-Children
Cassondra Windwalker

Meditations of a Beast
Kristine Ong Muslim

Little Joy

Matthew Murrey's *Little Joy* is a delight! He lovingly observes so many things that bring him joy: a swallow, a pigeon, an otter, a reddish finch, a cardinal, a "spindly-legged heron," a godwit, a refugee's first snow, red dancing shoes, a worn glove, a sudden downpour, garlic, basil, peonies, and papaya. He also tips his hat to Chicago, and to work, and how "time had worked us." There is beauty, and wisdom, and warmth, and love here. What more do you need?

—MATTHEW ROTHSCHILD
former editor & publisher of *The Progressive*

Like someone looking for a lost key, Matthew Murrey searches the world around him—an el platform in Chicago above a vacant lot, a hidden lake in the Northwoods of Minnesota, a blind man on a city street playing a black guitar for alms. What is it the poet seeks? A little joy? Yes, that must be it, for these poems leave us positively transported, transformed, transfixed by joy. This book is accomplished, lovely, and moving. What more might we ask of poetry?

—RICHARD JONES
author of *Passport*

Little Joy is a book of family, place, the lived world, and tenderness. The fans of Ted Kooser will gravitate to its plain-spoken human voice. I often sit with my coffee in the morning— / after writing in our sleeping house, after making / breakfast and lunches for my two boys, after looking at my wife's gentle chin— / and stare out the window, without speaking or writing / What would I say? How would I put it into words? Deftly, *Little Joy* puts into words the ineffable: the simple affections and questions that touch any life. Matthew Murrey speaks to readers, and readers will want to listen.

—JANICE HARRINGTON
author of *Yard Show*

In one poem in this book of prayers for finding joy in little things, Murrey quotes the photographer, Henri Cartier-Bresson, who claimed that "photography can fix eternity in a moment." This fixing is part of Murrey's project. But also, as the ecstatic poet William Blake wrote, one can find "eternity in a grain of sand." In these poems, Murrey looks straight on at the "grain"— the little things, like peonies and rain on a tin roof—to fix the joy, since, as he writes, "Tomorrow the grind . . . but not today."

—ATHENA KILDEGAARD
author of *Prairie Midden*

Little Joy

poems

Matthew Murrey

CORNERSTONE PRESS
UNIVERSITY OF WISCONSIN-STEVENS POINT

Cornerstone Press, Stevens Point, Wisconsin 54481
Copyright © 2026 Matthew Murrey
www.uwsp.edu/cornerstone

Printed in the United States of America.

Library of Congress Control Number: 2025950798
ISBN: 978-1-968148-32-4

Li-Young Lee, excerpt from "From Blossoms" from Rose.
Copyright © 1986 by Li-Young Lee. Used with the permission of The Permissions
Company, LLC on behalf of BOA Editions, Ltd., boaeditions.org.

Cornerstone Press titles are produced in courses and internships offered by the
Department of English at the University of Wisconsin–Stevens Point.

DIRECTOR & PUBLISHER   EXECUTIVE EDITORS
Dr. Ross K. Tangedal   Jeff Snowbarger, Freesia McKee

EDITORIAL DIRECTOR   SENIOR EDITORS
Brett Hill   Paige Biever, Reilly Crous

PRESS STAFF
Karlie Harpold, Abby Paulsen, Ryleigh Miller, Brian Grzesik, Sophie McPherson,
Sam Bjork, Madison Schultz, Autumn Vine

This one is for Carol Inskeep, my beloved partner, whom I have been lucky enough to be with for more than forty years—sharing both hard times and many, many little joys.

ALSO BY MATTHEW MURREY:

Bulletproof

P O E M S

– I –
HERE, WHERE I LAY DOWN

– II –
SCISSORS

– V –
PARADISE

There are days we live
as if death were nowhere
in the background; from joy
to joy to joy....

—Li-Young Lee, "From Blossoms"

– I –

HERE, WHERE I LAY DOWN

Swallow

If the swallow
had glanced up
from its flight
above the river,
it would have
seen me leaning
over the rail,
but it was pulling
a thread through my future;
it was dusting off
the kingdoms of the world;
it was humbling
the tyrant and the saint;
it was snapping
its beak across the back,
across the wings
of a tiny insect
which it carried off
to its mud nest
underneath the bridge.

The Rowboat

Thanks for leaving that rowboat
beside the little, hidden lake
in the north woods of Minnesota.
Steve and I found it flipped over
with two mismatched paddles
underneath. We turned it
and dragged it to the water.
It floated, so we paddled it out.
Lifting and pulling, we talked
about the years, how time had worked
us, how we'd become easier
on people, easier on ourselves.
We talked about love, a boat
that gets you there or gets swamped.
We talked about this earth—
the forest, the lake, animals we'd seen
and ones we'd only imagined.
Then we saw it and stopped:
something was swimming head-up
near the shore, swimming toward us.
We sat utterly still—paddles up, dripping—
as we watched its undulant body
trailed by a soft V of ripples unzipping the sky.
Minutes passed as it passed near, then away,
then out of sight. We decided it was an otter,
though it might have been a mink,
or something else. The whole morning
had the feel of a dream or folktale:
a little lake concealed in the woods,
an abandoned boat, the words we spoke,
the sudden apparition of an otter.
Back on shore, we dragged the boat
to where we'd found it, turned it over,
and tucked the paddles underneath.
I hope you don't mind that we borrowed it.

For the Joy, For Nothing

Below this concrete
and grated-steel bridge
that crosses the Chicago River
without ornament or elegance,
a pigeon is walking
along a strip of ground
between the river and Union Station.
Down there it's dirt
gravel and trash;
down there it's always
shadow and diesel smoke.
But the bird I'm watching
keeps walking,
searching, like someone
looking for a lost key.
Then she stops,
bends down, and picks up
a twig in her beak—a twig
here, where not a tree is in sight!
Her wings break into a blur
that lifts her
up from the ground,
then level with my eyes,
and finally into the yellow sunlight
shining above the station,
the river, the shadow,
and the smoke
where she picked and poked.
Then high in the air, she
wheels and flies three circles there
before heading north
upriver to her nest.
Three wide circles in the air
for the search, for what is found.

Cycling

(summer)
The way home is a gamble,
a roll of bruise-blue clouds
arching in from the west.
Faster, then a close flash
—bright foil and shine
just above the branches;
thunder lowers the boom.

(fall)
Wet socks, chilled face,
numb knuckles—how most
of the world lives slant
days of turning wind and rain.
My two tires spray gray water—
lick and spit of rubber on cement.
The poverty of getting there.

(winter)
Bundled and pedaling zero,
all is breath and brief sweat:
air a blade, my body a flame.
Rolling the frozen world,
I hear my heart and the wind
of my breath. Only ice
will bring me down.

(spring)
Reprieve: neither hurt
nor want. Chicory flowers
bring bits of sky to the ground.
Oak leaves are thin-skinned,
and—fast—I balance on tight air
like that little reddish finch there
who made it through somehow alive.

Vermin

In a box of books
I found their nest—
fluffed tufts of cloth,
pulled threads,
and shredded paper—
nestled in among stiff
covers, stamped spines,
and words enough
for little lifetimes. Yes,
there were scattered
dry, black bits of scat
and a sharp whiff of piss,
but what a tendered darkness
to curl up in for tiny dreams.

Inky

My son's rat is as clean
as a garden, as calm
as the Buddha's thumb.
When I hold him
he looks right at me,
but I'll never know
what he knows,
what any animal knows:
our dog staring out the window,
that cardinal on our roof
casting out his red song,
or the cows lining up
twice a day to be milked.
Most people think people
are completely different,
better than animals—
but I think of Inky the rat:
he's never bragged
of his patience,
bitten in anger,
or schemed after money.
I can't even say the same for myself.

Water on My Back, Chicago

Out of respect
I leave off my raincoat
as buildings of concrete, brick,
and stone darken
like a plowed field in the rain.
The streets shimmer and shush traffic
while sidewalks become sudden gardens
of opened umbrellas.
Here at the corner of LaSalle and Adams
I leave off my raincoat
as water gathers into small streams
which disappear through streetside drains
into the sightless roots of the city.
People passing can see
my backbone like a mole's trail
through my soaked shirt;
they can see me standing in the rain
like a spindly legged heron
shifting from foot to foot
and looking skyward now and then.
"Odd bird," some say to themselves,
but I am remembering that this city
once was marsh and prairie
with wet grass rustling in a blowing rain.

55th Street, Chicago

The puddles are glass eyes
fixed on the frozen copper sky.
From the El platform above
the vacant lot I hear the muffled
laughter and talk of men below.
Turning I see five men standing
around a fifty gallon drum of fire
the color of the sun's last yawn.

Today was too many dirty forks,
plates, and glasses to be washed.
Tired, I wasn't looking forward
to the long trip home. But then
only this: five men, a good fire,
talk, and laughter giving a voice
to the flames. Comfort. My train
arrives to take me home for the night.

Shifting

I was wind and sunlight again
on the El platform as a train pulled in.

Its doors opened to a woman
with wild, gray hair and loose layers

of mismatched clothes. Without one word
she tossed a blessing of birdseed for the birds

then pigeoned back from the closing doors.
I could call her crazy, but what about you and me

shifting for ourselves in our drabs and grays that hide
our iridescent purple and green fly-away dreams?

I wish I could wear my wings on my sleeve, even as I grub
for the money that gets me the food I need and the place I sleep.

Refugee Snow

Not shovels,
not the dread skid
to the ditch,
not even salt, no,
just childish rejoice
for their first ever,
for what's free,
falling and frozen,
yet floats like luck's feathers—
long flight from bad
to better, hunger
to dinner, cot to bed
and comforter.
It's contagious
this spontaneous
jump jump run and twirl,
this boy and this girl
with smiles up to taste
and palms out to catch
the sky falling:
fluffed tatters of icy white
that turn, on touching
skin, into a blessing of water.

Here, Where I Lay Down

There are trees. A tall one
that has shed all its leaves,
has its roots in my heart.
One, still bright with red
and orange, touches
the great loves of my life,
while a spruce, evergreen,
keeps me shamelessly naive.

All of us breathe,
and who can truly say
what color we are? Look
at the ground with all these
fallen leaves and you'll see
every shade under the sun.
To everything there is a season,
turn, turn. It's fall, so fall
for all of it: pity, love, the joke.

Tomorrow the grind—
debts, emails, the commute,
and bad news—but not today.
Today I am body and earth
in repose. Lines between dirt,
air, trees, and me are blurred.
The more I look, the less I know
where one ends and I begin.

Shamelessexuberance

The redbud can't contain itself—
blossoms breaking out
from the bark of its trunk and limbs.

A rooster two yards over
brags of his lust
as if his were the first.

Two squirrels swirl, frisk and twist
under a canopy
of apple flowers; they need

no tree of knowledge. And listen!—
wrens and crows
and creepers and jays and, and, and…

Even the dull backyard is now lush
in a blush
of violets trying to tint and tempt me

though these days have me
freighted with fretting. For shame.

Transfiguration

Baby, I'm bird, plant, wild-
flower. I'm a hothouse magnolia

and the fallen angel.
I am evo and emo, Adam

and Eve-o. I am so happy
in my artful Garden of Eden, oh!

Come feed my squirrels,
ransack my drawers,

read all my poems—
what's mine is yours.

Once I was a boring little boy,
and once I was even

an everyman, but—
for God's sake—I took a look

at so many books
and all was not lost,

but won: E pluribus unum
and all! Come celebrate with me

before ice melts, plants wilt,
and wildlife's gone.

Let's make a paradise
of this mess. Let's make saints

green with envy. Let's turn
everything green!

Here in this little hodgepodge
of heaven, I have been

transported, transformed, trans-
fixed by joy.

– II –

SCISSORS

Beauty Stopped Washing

and let her hair tangle.
At dinner she kept an eye
on him; he noticed her knife
and fork more and more left
untouched—hands and teeth
made do for tearing meat.
At first she'd talked so much,
but now returns his grunts
and snorts with her own

low snarls. The first bristles
felt odd, her tongue slipping out
to lick them. One day she quit
changing dresses; when it tore,
it was torn. Her nails went thick;
her mouth stuck out like a snout;
her arms and legs grew lean
as she roamed the house

on hands and feet. One night
after eating—the table a mess
of bones, their hands and chops
slick with blood and grease—
he growled as always, "Could you
love me?" She stared, stalked
to where he sat, and snarled,
a rough "Yes" against his neck,
then sprung off and sprinted
up the stairs. He followed her
to her once sumptuous room where
a shredded mattress and blankets

now made a musky nest. And there
they nipped and moaned and clawed
and whimpered and roared, taking
each other like animals in heat—
like beautiful beasts, like we.

The Red Shoes

I was supposed to be focused on the wafer turning flesh,
on the wine I once got drunk on becoming God's own blood,
but all I could think of were shoes—
my beautiful, brand new, shiny red shoes.

On my way out of Mass I heard the marble angel at the door
hiss, "Shame on you." I tapped my toes, clicked my heels,
and did a little two-step down the stairs.

Heading for home, I waltzed past the executioner's house.
Smirking, he squirted a bit of poison from his syringe,
sneered, "Come here, faggot, and I'll give you a stick."

A pair of red shoes is risky business. Everyone says,
"Wear something else!" Brown loafers, or white sneakers.
I think they envy my snazzy, red puppies;
see how they stare—even the saints turn to look.

You can spend your life down on your knees,
or standing in line, but I'll take these shoes any time—
the red ones: for dancing, for sissies like me.

Classical Guitar

Walking this evening
in my neighborhood I saw
the man whom I had heard
play Sor, Villa-Lobos, and Bach.
With his face as inscrutable
as Venus beneath the clouds,
his hands like suitors
had wooed the strings
in the five ways of love.
That guitar had sung
against his chest
like the night's first hour,
like a dozen red roses at the door,
like the fruit tree of Eden.
Tonight I only wanted
to say hello to him,
to tell him how much
I had enjoyed his performance.
But I knew that he would see
me staring at his hands,
at the naked curves of his finger-
tips. He would see my eyes
like tuning pegs turning,
tightening my thoughts to a pitch:
Oh, touch me, touch me
and make me sing!

Like That

A glove like that is not
for dressing wounds,
slicing bread, or helping
the dying bathe before bed.
It's not what you wear
to caress hair, touch
yourself, or make love.
Tough is what it is, for work
among planks and hammers,
blades and screws.
Despite stiff leather
and patches of worn shine,
there is something tender
in a glove like that. The hand
that labors inside it
may be cramped or stiff
by the end of the shift,
but comes out unscathed.
And maybe that hand
and glove have made something
like love: a snug doorframe,
a table to take the scrapes
and stains of countless meals,
or a floor where lovers
will dance or even lie down
and help each other out
of what covers them. Like that.

That Cosmopolitan Man

—Burt Reynolds, 1936–2018

Here is a bit of God
or Adam on the ceiling—
no, more ocher,
more shadow and flame
like sixteen-hundreds
Spanish or Dutch,
some painted saint
transfixed in firelight,
though in truth
it's just Burt in the buff;
all flesh and hair—
oh, those strokes
and hatches of hair!
Though dead, here he is
unfolding on his side
in loose recline again—
triptych of smoking grin,
muscles, joints, skin,
and all of that straight
and twisty black hair.
Here, he is the patron saint
of smooth temptation,
from tousled crown
to tender arch
nearly hidden in the dark.
Completely concealed
are his balls and dick
that no woman's magazine
could reveal back then.
Instead, Francesco Scavullo
had him slip one arm

snug between his thighs
so one is left to wonder.
I am full of wonder
for this sly masterpiece;
if only in my body
of work I am so lucky
as to leave behind
such a nakedness wanting
to be beheld—to be unfolded
and unfolded again.

Brancusi's *Sleeping Muse*

Ear to the ground,
oh mellow, brown-yellow
hollow orb, stay
still. Behind sealed lips
tongue hankers
for pancakes and kisses.
Missing hands miss everything:
keys, keyboards, hammers,
buttons, sand and silk.
And a long-lost dick—
well, you know
how pathetic dicks are,
don't you? Longing
fills the cask. Art
has turned my head
into the golden egg that lies
on the floor and listens
to exhaust and the chatter
of strangers who stop, stoop,
gaze, then walk away.
A thing of beauty is a joy, whatever.

Scrim

I still remember the wall
in *The Glass Menagerie*.
All it took was one light
to reveal Laura and her figurines,
another to hide her away.

Later that year, Willie Loman
going nowhere was suddenly
my father in his bent shoes,
getting in his car to go to work.
Another light, another dark.

We were sophomores when
Sister Ann Raymond took us
to the playhouse. I owe her—
and those amateurs inside
their characters, and the crews
who hammered the slats,
hung the painted cloths,
and aimed the lights.

Who would I be if I had missed
those plays with their scripts
like curtains, like gauze,
had missed those moments
when one light goes out
as another one comes on?

Scissors

In the beginning, you
cut the cord. When doors
first open, you snip
the ribbon. In a little kid's fist
you clip clumsy shapes.
For the seamstress you slip
through cloth like a shark.
At the scene of a wreck
you make quick work of wet,
red clothes and trim clean,
white strips of gauze.
Old Matisse took you up
and from painted paper cut
flowers, pomegranates, a vase.
Blake should've engraved you
in God's left hand,
severing the light from the dark,
innocence from all the rest.

Eleanor, Chicago 1953

—after Harry Callahan's photo

I love you, telephone pole,
brick streets, tracks,
and parked, fat cars.
Oh, back in the day,
my drab, sweet city.

Behind her, concrete
arches a roof and angles
to ramp a road. At her feet,
Neenah cast iron
covers another manhole,

while her face holds
the center and calls me to traffic
in black and white.
She fixes me with her stare.

Boys Running Into the Surf at Lake Tanganyika

—photograph by Martin Munkacsi, ca. 1930

I give you the water.

           I'll take it.

But I'll beat you to it.

Waves follow rules:
swell,   rise,   break.

I saw a photograph by your father
of three black children running into

Water, sun, naked
fun. The light's game,
the movement, the order and disorder—

           that lone hand
off to the left side.

Headlong, footsplash on sand, into the   breaking
wave's bright froth, the endless black and white

      of being alive—

that very photograph... was for me
the spark that set fire to the fireworks...
I suddenly understood
that photography can fix
eternity in a moment

muscle and grace and movement
here gather, and the wave of the moment
though it breaks,

is fixed.

Note: the statements in italics are those of Henri Cartier-Bresson
from his letters to Munkacsi's daughter.

The Black Guitar

Beneath the squared-off frame
of radiant sky and clouds,
among the angled, cornered shadows
leaning down, amid the dazzle
of light glanced, shook, and struck
off metal, glass, and polished stone,
within the multi-colored bustle
of the lunchtime crowd
reflected in plate glass windows—
I was stopped by sound,
a blind man playing a black guitar.
Wood, strings, and emptiness
humming black beneath his hands
closed my eyes for me,
while inside the splendid curvature
of my ears the city extended.
The traffic light clicked
above the blat of horns,
above the sputter and whir of engines.
Voices strolled out of
and into the hubbub afoot.
Overhead the El squealed and wailed,
steel wheels rasping steel rails.
And there before me, at the center,
was his music—like the light
that gives me the city I see.
I opened my eyes, dropped change
in his can, and walked away,
one exquisite city replacing the other,
fading like the music of the black guitar.
There have been times—standing
at a hurried corner or waiting

for a late train to arrive—
when I've closed my eyes and tried
returning to that invisible city,
but I always end up lost, lacking
what memory cannot provide:
the music as it really was.

Before the Dancers,

their shadows.
Before the fire, the hanging
breath. Before the kiss, the toss
and turn. Before the poem,
the page. Before death, sleep—
or was it death, then sleep?
Maybe I've had it wrong all along:
maybe the dancers, then their shadows.

– III–

WHERE THE ICE TOOK ME

In the Nostalgia Chair

I unfold Florida
days when I had my first
apartment, when I plugged in
a second-hand record player
and listened to my life.
It was small town, good
walking in the waking
morning while the sun
reinvented the horizon,
good night strolls
where stars kept track
above wires, leaves, and moss,
and churches were dark
empty, unlocked, and holy.
We had some times:
that night of wine, that morning
of coffee and rain. One time
we smoked and couldn't stop
laughing after we'd stared
at each other until you said
"I'm not feeling it."
And when I was alone
and holy, nights were for falling,
Look Homeward Angel, asleep.
That was a different state,
a thousand novels ago. It's a lie
to say I never looked back.
I still think about Keith Jarett
and the radio in the kitchen
and a bridge over a brown river
and a red-brick train station
and an afternoon of blue

thunder and broken branches.
Remember how the blinds
divvied up beauty on the wall
near the end of so many days,
and how green the world was
when we opened them? They
have fallen apart, like lovers,
like the loafers I wore when you left,
the ones, I'm sorry to say,
I threw away a long time ago.

Born in Winter in Florida

The bus thrummed under live oak and magnolia green
as I fell asleep and missed my stop. One time, lost

in a trance of smoke—*Camels* or *Players*—I swore I'd leave
my salty river and head north. Before I left, I watched

the thin squirrels and wondered what they knew; they
barked and scolded. I went to the river for a clue and ended
up with two fish to eat. That was no answer.

Years later, on the El, I fell asleep and woke to thieves
deciding I wasn't worth it. I could spend my life on what
might have been. I'll lie a little and say

I was born at high tide. I'll claim that I slipped in between
an assassination and a trip to the moon. That's not true
either. I had no control over any of it:

not the last-minute ride to the hospital, not the pink cry, not
the snowless, cold morning outside.

Manger

I have a soft spot
for the newly born,
the homeless, and the lost
looking up at the stars.
Forget judgement, the law,
and being born again;
this is all about straw,
sheep, and a place to sleep.
In early December my mother
would unpack the trim,
little wooden shed she'd
sawed and nailed together.
In it she'd pose the plaster angels,
animals, and gathered humans.
I am done with any hope
not born of this world, but I'll stop
in silence to look at a crèche:
animals at rest, tired shepherds
kneeling, elegant sojourners
holding gifts, little exiled family,
and my mother like God
fixing one bright star above it
on a strand of fishing line
so thin it was almost invisible.

My Solstice

I was born to the darkest month
when many go looking for light.
I have driven far at night
for roofs, trees, and hedges
hung with lights—white,
green, yellow, red, and a blue
so blue it refuses focus.
Yes, to long nights, and yes
to the bushes, branches, and eaves
that you were so moved to grace
with all the little jewels of your lights.

Where the Ice Took Me

One time I caught my mother
slam-slinging bottles into a garbage can—
the clear and green shattering, a music
she could not resist.

This morning puddles were glassed
with ice as I biked to work, so I rode right
over as many as I could, busting
apart the freezing quiet and falling

forty winters and a thousand miles back
to Florida, a playground, and a rare, hard freeze.
In uniforms and stiff black shoes, we sprinted
iced puddle to puddle, stomping them, splintering

their brittle lids—as if the sound of all
that breaking were the sound of breaking free.

Cacao, Chicago

Chocolate is this winter morning
on the Michigan Avenue Bridge.
Below, a boat cracks open the river.
Above, the Wrigley Tower lifts
time like a gift to the gray sky.
West, upwind, the chocolate factory
is pouring steam into the air.
I huddle on the bridge and inhale
the bittersweet air that breaks
in my nose and makes my mouth go moist.

Threading North and South

31 frayed my nerves pulling over
in the middle of nowhere
Michigan every thirty miles to pour
water into the hot, leaky radiator.

45 took us south into ninety degrees
of July and a battlefield nearby
before we slipped like wounded
ghosts into Mississippi for the night.

17 was awfully pretty skirting
the river as it wound its way
from the city where I grew up
to my first home away from home.
And I never moved back.

In my twenties I headed north
and I'll never forget my first trip
south on 41 with the oceanic
lake to my left and the giant teeth
of skyscrapers ahead. I grinned
like a kid seeing mountains
or snow for the first time.

I love the blocked, black
numbers on white shields;
they conjure up slowing down—
tobacco sheds, red bricks, a river,
a bean field, intersections and signs:
Open, Closed, Vacancy.

Sometimes it's fences to the west,
or waking up to see what the clouds
are up to and how many miles are left.
Sometimes it's speeding to get there
before nightfall, and hoping—that dark
or not—the lights will be on as they should be.

Remembering Fire

Outside the air had left its brittle, white breath
on metal and leaves and grass while my three sisters and I slept warm
under wool. Our father woke us for school. We took our clothes in hand
and ran to the only warm room, the living room which pulsed

in the light from the fireplace. We stood with our stomachs facing the fire,
then turned laughing red and hot-faced at our shadows swaying
huge and silent on the wall. Finally, we held our clothes up
to the fire and put them on when they were hot and smelled like ironing.

I woke this morning in the dark chill of our apartment just as the furnace
was switching on. I heard the clank and the hiss of the radiators, time's
machinery shifting; heard my father on hands and knees
in the other room blowing the flames, stoking the fire.

Standing By

Detroit, halfway, I waited
for my flight that wouldn't leave
for over an hour. A woman
was working the gate,
took worries and questions.
"Is this my flight?" *It is.*
"Do I need to check-in?" *No,*
you have your boarding pass.
She smiled, was polite, even bent
down to distract a crying baby,
What a sweetie, how old?
When she left, she passed
so close that I could see where
her makeup ended, could see
the hair-sprayed brushstrokes
in her hair. The ironed creases
in her pants were almost gone,
the back of her blouse wrinkled.
I noticed her foot: strapped
in a dark-blue shoe, closed at the toe
and open at the back. She wore
a thin, black sock, and her foot
tilted, sagged off to the side
like an old tire gone soft. My feet,
too, are a bit off kilter: each shoe
wears out on the heel's edge
though I can never recall
walking that way. My father also
was on his feet too much; his work
shoes wore out lopsided
from walking the length
of a loud, lousy bar every day.

Sometimes his leg would cramp
so tight he'd wake up yowling,
and it would wake us. We'd hear
the muffled soothe of my mother,
calm as a medic, talking him through it
while she held and kneaded
the back of his leg, loosening
that fist of muscle that struck
as he slept and left him like a boy,
begging for the mercies.

Bigger Than Your Hand

My job's on the third floor,
top floor, so the ceiling
is nothing but the underside
of the roof. Sometimes
at work I have orders
to finish, a lesson to prepare,
and no time to find
the missing books.
At other times no one
shows up, the screens
all go black,
and I sit with the fact
that the time of my life
is passing away for good.

I like the windows at work,
especially when gray-blue
clouds come in thick
from the west, dimming
the day. What's best
is when I forget them,
then hear it: sudden
white noise of a downpour
sheeting the roof, shushing
the library. Think wind,
and leaves caught up in it,
or a waterfall you can't see
for the trees, or the ocean
forever rushing the shore,

or that wider, deeper ocean
you first heard when

you were little and someone
handed you a shell
bigger than your hand,
and you lifted it
to your ear and listened.

Tin

Back then she worked in a warehouse
with a tin roof. One time she took me with her,
must have been the year before I started school.
I played on the floor while she sat typing fast
at an electric typewriter that seemed bigger than I was.
Before lunch, there was thunder, then a downpour;
both of us stopped, looked up. What an uproar,
as if a thousand of my mothers were up there
banging away on typewriters in a fury of work.

Bridge

On my way to work I've stopped
mid-span to smell chocolate
cooking in a factory to the west,
then turned away and shivered
while the river below flowed
unseen beneath a skin of ice.

I've leaned on railings
in the middle of nowhere
to watch swallows swoop
and swirl as they snatched
insects out of the air—
a slow river reflecting
those hungry maneuvers.

And maybe the saddest soul
in the world can be turned
back from the dizzying edge
by the grace of one bird
or the light of the magic hour.

They say life is short,
still, we have to go to work—
cooking, serving, typing,
building. Even the roughest
of us stops on a morning
like this to lean on the railing
and wash their face in the gold
like that fellow tossing crusts
for the birds in the air
and the ones in the water below.

– IV–

THE DEVOTIONS

Little Laughing Buddha

In his left hand he's holding something aloft:
a rock? a plum? a pickled egg? I have no time
for glum Buddhas declaring the world's but a scrim—
an illusion good for nothing but scorn.
But this one's all right. He knows the emperor
is full of shit. He knows what brutes soldiers are—
how they make old men scream; what they do
to girls. He knows what an ass his neighbor is,
the one who says, "All's well at home; all's well in the realm."
He knows time is short, the sun does not conspire,
and the cricket sings no lies. He holds his hand aloft
and laughs a mouth-wide-open belly laugh
that's disarming and infectious—though I'm never quite sure
what on Earth is so funny, what it is he's laughing about.

Garden of Love

—Nuremberg Tapestry, 1460

Women and men and pork and port
and bread. The looks, the lute,
red lips, and green leaves. Flowers,
a table, braids, and white smocks.
It's heaven, but there I am,
the one on the left with *that* look
on her face: worry spoiling like mold
in the dough. What about the castle,
the bishop, the soldiers? I think of
unlit torches waiting for fire, honed
blades in their scabbards, and crates
of bloodless bolts, their crossbows
taut and silent. You fill my goblet,
fill the room with laughter, and invite me
to shake off my gloom with a song.

What I Did on a Rainy Day

Left tracks across the floor.
Eyed the pillows and the sheets.
Saw the world as a cloud,
then wiped my glasses clean.
Did not cry.
Did not complain.
Did not harm the grass.
Did not turn the dirt over.
Dry beneath a roof,
I lay down to listen,
and counted myself
among the luckiest souls
alive under the sun,
which was nowhere to be seen.

Arc

Rain takes the clouds apart,
leaves the trees a darker dark.
Fallen leaves fall apart,
old news in roads and yards.
My breath, that threadbare scarf,
leaves my lips and falls apart.
Who hates fall's end, winter's start—
the coming snow, the swelling dark?
Not the tulip bulb, not my heart.
In winter's bed, cold and harsh,
dream of summer's wild, green art.

Spice

I've cursed God countless times,
but I have heaven
by the tips of my fingers,

fragrant from pinching basil's
flowering spikes, plucking
a colander of its heady leaves.

Not just basil, but garlic's holy oil
anoints my three fingers that pressed
the cloves to the cutting board.

Bless the perfumes of the earth, and bless
my blasphemies; they are the fresh
ground pepper gracing the finished dish.

Rust and Sweat

Next to the lilac,
the old reel mower
is motionless, its stiff
handle angled up.
I like its faded
red metal parts
speckled with rust.
I like how the grass
has been growing
through the blades
and the cutting bar
since the last time
I used it. Tomorrow
it'll be over there
near the garden,
or beside the woodpile,
and the grass
will be shorter,
and the wooden grip
on the mower
will be a shade
darker and shinier
where I held it
with both hands
as I pushed it
back and forth across
an hour of my life.

The Devotions

The apple at lunch caught my eye
when a bite I took went right to the core

and exposed the little monastic seeds,
one with its brown-black jacket split

by the thin tendril of a new root
fruitlessly probing the flesh for dirt.

Outside it was March—skeletal
trees, shaded frost, sackcloth of grass.

Finished, I tossed the gnawed core
into the trash. It landed with a loud clunk

like an abbot's knock on a monk's door,
and interrupted my brief imitation of prayer.

Ripe

In the dead apple tree
there was one striking red
cardinal flitting branch to branch.

Afterlife

No more for the climbing;
nor for the praise of beauty.
Fallen and stark they are
beneath the lifted arms
of the breathers at their
green work in the day's light.
Some by rot, soft-hearted fell.
Some were sheared and snapped,
or dropped roots and all
by a fierce and merciless wind.
Some like saints died standing
becoming their own gravestones.

Most of us pass here in wonder
of the green roof, the leaf and
limb works, and the sturdy trunks.
But today my mind is on the ones
who will not add another ring,
who have retired from the sun
to lie down among the ferns
and the youngest trees. The ones
who have given their bodies over
to the long-fingered fungi,
to the mouthwork of ants and grubs,
to the bracelets and rings of bacteria:
that soft heaven of the hungry soil.

This Spring the Peonies

Because they stand up against the kingdom of snow.
Because they let the lilac and iris bloom first.
Because even the mean of spirit have them in their yards.
Because they are white, crimson, purple and pink.
Because they die back to the ground in the fall.
I have dragged myself from bed at four in the morning.
I have endured the winter of lost words and phrases.
I have made promises of love and devotion to the peonies.
I have sworn to be faithful to them in my little songs.

Heat

Like the stronger brother, it humbles us.

A judge wipes his brow and reaches for a glass of water
as a darkness spreads its wings
across the shoulders of the lawyer and the accused.
Big men sit down in shade and say nothing.
Little birds stay quiet, keep to shadows
like children in church.

Last night I stood at my sink washing bowls and spoons;
I was stripped to the waist and sweat beaded from my skin
as if I had swallowed a bit of sun.
I liked standing there—trickles of sweat, reminders
that in the end it all belongs to the sun:
trees, hungry leaves, cicadas, fog in the morning,
the moon swelling up over the horizon, and me
warm and dripping like the first man standing up
from a stream, like the last man reduced to tears.

The Strange Cabinet
—Mexico City, 1986

I woke up a thousand miles gone
with my skin simmering, with a cape
of ache draped on my shoulders.
My stomach kept nothing down.

From bed I teetered up
and zombied down the street
to a little *tienda*, where I stared
at slices of bright papaya,
and said *quisiera, quisiera*—
I would like, I would like—
pointing at one peppered with seeds.
Si, si, con las semillas, por favor—
Yes, yes, with the seeds, please.

Twenty-five years on,
I can still taste the bite
of the cure—bitter, black pearls.
Back in my room I fell back
into bed where I twisted and
sweat-dreamed one more day:
the sheet was ocean, pillows
three countries I could not save.

I did get better; thank you bitterness.
But I've never eaten papaya again,
and the memory's now blurred
like one of those burning dreams.

Was that really me, or some sleepwalker
staggering through a choppy, silent film

before the real nightmares began?
Maybe I was never in Mexico.
Maybe I never left home. Maybe
I just fell asleep at the movies
and was too young to understand.

Buoyancy

I strip step in lie down
and am born again
in another soak I begin
with what I walk on lightly
abrade the pads of my feet
and toes with the light
grit of a pumice stone
done I sit up to soap
my armpits with their scent
and scribbles of hair
then lather my back and chest
wondrous hub of moving air
and blood which I follow
sudsing up my neck
to my face until I have to
shut my eyes the way
it must have been the morning
I was born the way I did
when I first learned to pray
here I am as close to prayer
as I'll ever get now holy
holy holy every body
I rinse to resee the world
and stand to finish soaping
belly then down to my soft
furred sex that has been good
to me as has been my butt
rounded and divided and doing
the heavy lifting and the dirty
work I give it a good kneading
before working my way down
my legs that start out solid

enough but soon are so thin
bones muscles and skin
that have walked me through
my life done down I go recline
into the warm uplift one more time
then flip the drain and listen
as the water descends
and all my heavy returns

– V –

PARADISE

Long Into the Night

This house I love best
with its lights still on at five a.m.
and voices in the living room:
a man and a woman talking.

They have talked past the radio
stopping into static,
past the tired neighbors
latching their doors,
past the last dog barking.

I don't care whether they're
brother and sister,
old friends, or lovers.
Their voices please me
like the light from their windows
which I watch from here,
brindled in streetlight and tree shadow,
with my shoulder sack of newspapers
and two dozen silent houses still to go.

Slumbers

These two want to wait up for Mama,
but I lull them with books, sleep
them down with warmth and words.

Their heads on my biceps and shoulders,
they breathe down to drowse.
I father them across the way horizon
brings night, the way a leaf
gives its shadow to shade.
The easy pace of our breaths
lays them out loose-limbed in sleep's sprawl.

Lying there, eyes closed, I listen and fall
under the sway of the same drowsy drug
as—tables turned—my sons breathe me,
float me like waves, down to my own tired sea.

Map to the Moon

That is the dream I had
when I was stuck in that little town,
wishfully watching planes in the sky,
thumbing the atlas all the time.

I dreamed I'd go to the purple
city and find you. I believed
that lights would turn on
in the tall buildings to welcome me.

And I did go,
though I took an overnight train
that rolled in after sunrise and took me
past the stadium and brick warehouses
and apartments with shades drawn.

And there was a river
and a bridge, and at night a yellow
brilliance at the center which I wanted
as a moth wants the light
it flings itself at over and over.
And you were there,
which is why memory paints it
so lovely, so purple, so speckled—
even prettier than it really was—

and tells a little lie about how young
the moon was, when everybody
knows it's older than dirt
and that love is the youngster.
That was decades ago,
but I remember falling
like it was yesterday. So yes,
the night and moon were young,
and my heart waxed full.

Constellations

I was close. A little snow
on the ground. Stars
out. No moon. The sky laughed
so faintly I barely heard it
and cupped my ears to be sure.
It came again—a little louder:
geese. I'd never seen them after dark,
but recalled a poem by Jimmy Carter:
on the roof of the White House
one night he heard
and watched a string of geese
crossing our capital's starless sky.
I looked up to see,
and soon they passed over me:
a handful in loose formation leading,
then a trailing line,
then the honking V coming last.
They numbered about thirty,
high up and dimly lit by ground light;
they were like faint stars,
like a constellation on the move,
sliding south and west of Orion
so the trailing V crossed the V of Taurus' horns.
Then I lost them, but could still hear
their calling out to one another.
That sound usually leaves me sorry
for myself, wanting to fly away,
yet going nowhere; but tonight
hearing them high in the dark, flying far
in this freezing air, made me happy
to be walking down here, almost home.

In the Thick of It

These young poets on love:
you'd think it was all
in the hands, the pivot
and slide, necks, beds,
beads of sweat and sweet
cum's perfumes—
which it is, though
we have other
things to tell them.
Above the door, the clock
needs a battery. A cloak
of dust dulls the framed
couple. A sink
of dishes waits for bare
hands. I dare them
to include electricity
bills, evening meetings
with teachers, trips
to the emergency room,
the fifth inning again,
the dryer tumbling, and grass
that never stops growing.
Oh, it is also night,
the children asleep and
the bedsprings singing
and the Lord's name taken
wholly and lusciously in vain.

Smoke

In first grade, the sisters told us
of Cain and Abel heaping their fires,
hoping the smoke would make God
smile. Abel's rose, but Cain's
hugged the ground like fog
which made him smolder, hot
to shed his brother's blood—odd
story to tell a roomful of kids.

In ninth grade, home alone, I found
my sister's pack of Marlboro Lights,
pulled one out—sweet nail—and lit it.
I sat by the fireplace so I could blow
that grey, blue smoke up the flue
where it would rise over the roof, to God
knows where. A dizzy, sexy buzz
fogged my brain, felt damn good.

Sometimes my wife and I come home
and smell that skunky, pungent odor
from behind their door. Godlike,
the law condemns, but we turn blind eyes.
They're growing up, those two, our sons.
They were boys once, and bitter foes,
but now they smoke together. Time
burns many ways. Their childhood
has passed; we smell it, burned to ash.

Drunk in the Basil

Not drunk, just tipsy. A plump bumble bee
straddles a spike of delicate basil blossoms
and plants its face in the flowers, sucking in
what is sweet, while I keep plucking leaves
and breathing in the spice—stopping now
and then for one more swallow of wine:
one for you and me, one for the sun
gone behind the roof already, one
for these first leaves to have lost
their green, and one for this
final full colander
of the season.
I rise
and
raise
this
glass
to
the
pain
in my knees
and to the gods
of the dirt; they understand.

I Walked into the Fire Pit

in the backyard last night
because I was taken
with the sky, the crisp
stars in the chill air—
first cold snap of the year.
I was carrying scraps
to the compost pile
and forgot about the steel,
black fire pit in the yard.
My shinbone—thick
as the shaft of a spear—
hit it hard, but I didn't fall,
didn't drop all the scraps.
I did do a little hop dance
to the silent music of pain
and mouthed lyrics of curse
at myself for being
so goddamned clueless,
though—to be honest—
I was kind of amused
at the busted Magoo
of myself. I bent down to soothe
my hurt, and—hunched like that
beside that black fire pit
with not a bit of fire in it—
I turned my head
and glanced at the sky
again, blackness flecked
with such an embarrassment
of fine and bright specks of light
that I once again was struck
by the cold comfort of the sight.

Paradise

Twenty years ago, I set off to find her
in fields, cities, libraries, woods, and museums.
Everywhere I went, I took my little notebook
and scribbled down descriptions, impressions
and clues. I was a regular private eye.

Every morning before work, I worked
on them, and slowly they came—
short and long, of love and despair, clever
and simple, a few I still don't understand.
But she was always two steps ahead.

All these years later, I'm like that fellow
in the Jewish tale who just walks away
from his boring village and the drudgery
of work, children and wife—sets off
for Paradise. Halfway there,
asleep at night, he gets turned around
by an imp (or angel) so when he arrives
right back where he started, he's not sure
where the hell he is—heaven
or home, earth or Paradise!

I often sit with my coffee in the morning—
after writing in our sleeping house, after making
breakfast and lunches for my two boys,
after looking at my wife's gentle chin—
and stare out the window, without speaking or writing.
What would I say? How would I put it into words?

Not Paris

Finally in Paris,
in a restaurant, in the first summer
after 9/11, I saw on the wall a faded poster
for a concert in July 1984, that long gone summer
I was going to travel abroad
for the first time in my life.

I had dictionaries and money saved
from waiting tables, but I was torn. Young,
devout, and done with college, I believed Jesus
didn't want me to wait any more, but wanted me
to give everything away and go live among the poor,
so that's what I did: a shelter in Chicago instead of a flight
delayed for eighteen years.

That poster was a little door
to old dreams of hostels and hitchhiking and waking up
on a train from Germany to France. When I saw it,
such an emptiness emptied me sitting there, it felt as if
I might never get up. Then I thought of you

and cigarettes on the back stoop
and soup steaming in big pots and cards in the basement
after dark and the sharp, damp smells of too many people crowded
in one big room to sleep. There's nothing more holy than the heart
on the sleeve, how we met. Yes,

that's what I did. Not Paris
our years near Lake Michigan with its ice
and horizon, or our seasons beside the slow, narrow Iowa River,
or the long, rough birth of our first which almost came
to nothing but blood, or the easier one of our second,

born in the little city—middle of nowhere, Illinois
with its town-sized farms of corn and soy and its muddy creeks—
where we stayed.

I looked at that poster again
and marveled at the itineraries I never expected,
then got up from my table to pay the bill, to struggle with my poverty
of French so I could say *The food was good* and *Goodbye*.
Yes, I did get up—of course I did—but for all the detours
and everything missed, I forgave myself,
and blessed myself, too.

Godwit

I'm thinking of it flying with no rest
for five and a half days over the ocean
that might as well be infinity
for one so small and only halfway there.

One time flying, I was halfway there
and from the safety of my seat
looked seven miles down
to see nothing but sea.
The huge airplane that carried us
was but a strand of hair, or needle
against the vastness down there.

A godwit weighs not a pound,
yet flies eleven days without cease
across seven thousand miles of sea
before reaching the southern bay
where it is summer, not the winter
I cannot leave. I warm to it,

the journey long on promise
and risk, no maps or guarantees—
just water, wind, sun and the certain
stars every clear night until it ends.

Four Lights

Each point lit its spot
in an arc that was easy
to sight across the dark sky.
At the west end bright, white
Venus descending, while rising
rust-orange in the east, Mars
gleamed like the embered end
of a stick pulled from a fire.
Between them, us,
and in that trace of sky
east to west, dim Saturn
then Jupiter almost twinning
Venus's shine. That is how
summer ended—one son
had his bags packed;
his brother wasn't so sure.
For a couple minutes
we stood at the edge
of the meadow and looked up
at that necklace of worlds
and then went home
to our little place in the wonder.

ACKNOWLEDGMENTS

Grateful acknowledgment is given to the editors who published these poems, sometimes in earlier versions or under different titles.

The 2River View: "Paradise"
Anthropocene: "Manger" and "Shifting"
Apple Valley Review: "Tin"
Artful Dodge: "Heat"
Bear Review: "The Devotions"
Calliope: "Long into the Night"
Cultural Weekly: "Brancusi's Sleeping Muse" and "Inky"
The Dodge: "The Rowboat"
Escape Into Life: "Constellations," "Four Lights," "I Walked into the Fire Pit," and "Like That"
HAD: "Spice"
The Ekphrastic Review: "Eleanor, Chicago 1953"
Florida Review: "Classical Guitar" and "Remembering Fire"
The Inflectionist Review: "Before the Dancers,"
Journal of the American Medical Association: "The Strange Cabinet"
Kansas Quarterly: "Cacao, Chicago" and "55th Street Chicago"
the lickety~split: "Ripe"
Manoborn: "What I Did on a Rainy Day"
Midwest Quarterly: "Swallow"
One: "Standing By"

ONE ART: "Scrim" and "Arc"
Painted Bride Quarterly: "Water on My Back, Chicago"
Poet & Critic: "For the Joy, for Nothing"
Poetry East: "Where the Ice Took Me"
Poets Reading the News: "Refugee Snow"
Rattle: "In the Nostalgia Chair," "Map to the Moon," and "Threading North and South"
The Shore: "Rust and Sweat"
Sleet: "Boys Running into the Surf at Lake Tanganyika"
Spillway: "Beauty Stopped Washing"
Spoon River Poetry Review: "The Black Guitar"
Sticks: "This Spring the Peonies"
Sweet: "Smoke"
Tar River Poetry: "Scissors"
Under a Warm Green Linden: "Godwit" and "In the Thick of It"
Wilderness: "Afterlife"

"Refugee Snow" also appears in the anthology, *Voices on the Move: an Anthology by and about Refugees* (Solis Press, 2020)

* * *

I want to thank Richard Jones, poet and editor of *Poetry East,* who was incredibly kind and encouraging to me decades ago when I was just a few years into being a poet. It also has been much more than a little joy to work with Dr. Ross K. Tangedal, director and publisher of Cornerstone Press, Karlie Harpold, amazing student editor, Abby Paulsen, cover designer of this book, and the other student editors who kindly read and helped improve these poems. Finally, I'd like to thank Sam Bjork and Sophie McPherson for their critical work in the sales and media promotion of *Little Joy*.

Matthew Murrey is the author of *Bulletproof*, chosen by Marilyn Nelson for the Jacar Press 2018 poetry competition. A National Endowment for the Arts recipient, Murrey's work has appeared in dozens of journals, including *Midwest Quarterly, Split Rock Review, Poetry East,* and others. He was a public school librarian for over twenty years and lives in Urbana, Illinois.